Furious Lullaby

Crab Orchard Series in Poetry *Editor's Selection*

Furious Lullaby

OLIVER DE LA PAZ

Crab Orchard Review

&

Southern Illinois University Press

CARBONDALE

Printed in the United States of America

10 09 08 07 4 3 2 1

The Crab Orchard Series in Poetry is a joint publishing venture of Southern Illinois University Press and *Crab Orchard Review.* This series has been made possible by the generous support of the Office of the President of Southern Illinois University and the Office of the Vice Chancellor for Academic Affairs and Provost at Southern Illinois University Carbondale.

Crab Orchard Series in Poetry Editor: Jon Tribble

Library of Congress Cataloging-in-Publication Data
De la Paz, Oliver, 1972–
Furious lullaby / Oliver de la Paz.
p. cm.— (Crab Orchard Series in poetry)
ISBN-13: 978-0-8093-2774-4 (pbk. : alk. paper)
ISBN-10: 0-8093-2774-0 (pbk. : alk. paper)
I. Title. II. Series.

PS3554.E114F87 2007
811'.6—dc22 2007001578

Printed on recycled paper. ♻

The paper used in this publication meets the minimum requirements of American National Standard for Information Sciences—Permanence of Paper for Printed Library Materials, ANSI Z39.48-1992. ∞

FOR MEREDITH

The exceeding brightness of this early sun

Makes me conceive how dark I have become . . .

—WALLACE STEVENS

Aye, on the shores of darkness there is light.

—JOHN KEATS

Contents

THREE

Acknowledgments

Grateful acknowledgment is made to the readers and editors of the following publications, in which these poems, sometimes in slightly different versions, first appeared:

Columbia: A Journal Literature of and Art—"My Dearest Regret"
Controlled Burn—"Aubade with Starlings and Kerosene Muted by Glass"
Crab Orchard Review— "On the Motions of Death," "Aubade with a Thistle Bush Holding Six Songs," and "Epitaph for the Musculature of the Neck"
CRATE—"My Dearest Apostasy" and "Fury"
Dickinson Review—"What the Dead Said" and "What the Eye Said"
The Drunken Boat—"Widening Aubade" and "Aubade with a Heel of Bread, a Heart, and the Devil"
From the Fishouse—"Hour of Dawn" and "Messengers"
Hayden's Ferry Review—"God Essay" and "Prayer Essay"
Image: Art, Faith, Mystery—"Aubade with Constellations, Some Horses, and Snow"
L.A. Review—"On the Fenestra Ovalis"
North American Review—"On the Epidermis" and "Aubade with the Moon, Some Bones, and a Word"
Painted Bride Quarterly—"My Dearest Conflict"
Passages North—"Aubade with a Book and the Rattle from a String of Pearls"
Pleiades—"What the Ear Said"
Runes—"Aubade with Memory Crystallized into a Figure of a Dancer"
Siren—"Flutter," "Hush," "Constricting Aubade," and "Aubade with Scorpions and Monsoon"
Sonora Review—"The Devil's Book"
Sou'wester—"Holiness"
Vespertine—"Aporia"

"Aubade with a Book and the Rattle from a String of Pearls," "Aubade with a Thistle Bush Holding Six Songs," "Aubade with Memory Crystallized into a Figure of a Dancer," "My Dearest Recklessness," and "My Dearest Regret" appear in *Poetry 30: Thirtysomething American Thirtysomething Poets*. Edited by Dan Crocker and Gerry LaFemina, published by Mammoth Books in 2005.

"Aubade with Bread for the Sparrows" appears in *Contemporary Voices from the Eastern World: An Anthology of Poems*. Edited by Tina Chang, Nathalie Handal, and Ravi Shankar, published by W.W. Norton and Company in 2007.

I give thanks to Western Washington University, Utica College, Northern Michigan University, and Gettysburg College for their support. A poetry fellowship from the New York Foundation for the Arts was also of invaluable help. Finally, I am grateful to my wife, Meredith, and friends and mentors Alberto Ríos, Beckian Fritz-Goldberg, Norman Dubie, Jeanne E. Clark, Eugene Gloria, Nick Carbó, Denise Duhamel, Sarah Gambito, Jon Pineda, Joseph Legaspi, Paolo Javier, Bino Realuyo, Rick Barot, Rigoberto González, Aimee Nezhukumatathil, Patrick Rosal, Barbara Jane Reyes, Camille Dungy, Jon Tribble, Allison Joseph, Austin Hummell, Steve Scafidi Jr., Evelina Galang, Fred Leebron, Kathryn Rhett, Bruce Beasley, Suzanne Paola, Brenda Miller, Eileen Tabios, April Ossmann, Adrian Matejka, Stacey Lynn Brown, Sue Allspaw, Papatya Bucak, Mary Kenagy, Argie Manolis, and Rodney Jones, who I forgot to thank in my hurry last time.

One

Holiness

The first word in our catechism was "holy,"
and we would march up the aisle, boys matched with girls,
our hands folded while we soaked in grace from the blue
light of stained glass. We were a river of blessings.

I wanted to be "holy," and I had practiced
my prayers before a mirror until I looked like a statue
or a ghost. No one could deny me this office
and I walked with my eyes toward the altar.

No one drifted. No one held their breath.
I didn't have visions of angels then.
I could only hold my place, keeping my chin up
as if I were swimming. What else is there to know

about divinity? What else is there to know
about the poverty of a word?

Hour of Dawn

The light covers us with little tongues,
making us conscious of bed sheet texture.

We hold ourselves in contempt.

Our bodies coax a story sunrise
cannot disrupt as shade passes.

Then morning—we think only
of the honeysuckle, the cedar
the trembling aspen,
its bark, a sepulcher-white moment.

In the low dream, we turn and break . . . our bodies
rise and breathe.

The hour of dawn holds us still.
We still our lungs. Eyelids clench
facing the sun and we fade.

Our skins warmed away from dormancy,
gleam, star-like and far.

We are gathered back into the things of this world
and turn away from the sore-red sun, moved
to deny who we will be when we are awakened.

Aubade with Scorpions and Monsoon

Little sleeper, I mentioned the scorpions
were thoughtless in the rain, as they swam down

the length of the green skins to the flood, eel-like
with furious tails. Earlier, the sky

had turned a mustard color proving that August
and its rains would soon bathe the desert, making

the whole thing become a dark scar. Water caused
the scorpions to shelter against the cacti

spikes. Their yellow-brown exoskeletons
click-clacked as they climbed atop one another,

preserving themselves. Of course the cacti
were indifferent to all this as are you

when you are sleeping. How calamitous
it would be to miss your slumber. I know

it's early and daybreak is just another
accident sufficient for us to snub

in our weariness. Listen, the monsoon's
relentless. The lightning leapt from cloud

to cloud in whole valleys. It looked like
a flashlight shined on the rafters

of the firmament. What an astonishment
to see the desert take on water in starved

portions. However, your god is sleep
and it's difficult to admonish one

so calm and white. You're like a chalcedony
street on a Sunday. Listen, this is hard

and I'd hate to wake you just to tell you
the scorpions held each other by their pincers

until dawn, spiraling down the saguaros in amber rosettes.
Hush. There are torrents above our heads

and sleep is a phantom thing for us to hold.

Constricting Aubade

The geese are a dark purple as they pass over the lake.
There are too many crystals glinting in the early sun
which blind the fliers but not enough to throw them.

The arms of the formation remind you of a schoolmate
who was born with a deformed left hand,
the thumb and small finger stretched outward
with three missing middle digits.

You are frightened by this memory
as one who happens upon a machinery accident.

The shadows of the flock burn
their arrows over the ground in their haze and yours.

The winter comes. The early memory of the child with the hand
plows past the horizon. The grasses along the lake
will grow frantic and freeze. Soon you will wake me
and tell me the story of the geese, how they sounded
like small voices in a storm.

Flutter

Listen, their lungs are terrible and they perch on power lines, ready
to pause at our doorstep. Ash-mouthed and mischievous,
their wicked beaks full of hair. If we kept disintegrating

into the sound of wings, we would be shoeboxes of dust by morning.
Even now their eyes are holes. And in that parliamentary space
just so above the ground, caws of a final trespass.

The skies are white at this hour. The first frost enters
the kitchen glazing a porcelain mug, making the apparition
of a mug on the counter. Bone light streams like angels of the nativity

and we busy ourselves gathering bits like they often do: spoons into
drawers,
the gold band of a wrist watch. We stagger to get half-dressed, change
keeps us moving. So many clothes emptied and worn

and emptied again. Wasn't it always like this—ourselves denuded
in increments, the unbuttoned blue shirt, the rush to shoes
scuffed upon each other—wasn't this the way we lived?

We let go. We count everything. Cut the chrysanthemum
stems at a slant, place the vase on the ledge in sunlight,
fill the dog bowl with kibble. When it rains, we are rained upon.

When it snows will we have the difficulty of remembering gardens
or the answer to what it was we were traveling for? White rows
of houses blur, window frame after window frame. Occasionally a child

makes faces out the window. Our eyes come to rest on this bit. It is
something
to keep us hushed as when walking through a field to a cottonwood
forest
filled with crows about to fly, one footstep bursts them into the bright
inevitable air.

Aubade with Doves, a Television, and Fire

The gunwales of a ship at sea are on fire
and the fact that something in water blazes
keeps us awake for hours. At the edge of the boat
people jump over the railing, braving both
the flames and water. Still,

in the screen glare we catch
the way we sleep in summer.
No shoulder between us
can say this deeply. The ship
bleeds off the television's edge
like a thief. The captain is a handsome man

who kept a dovecote next to the life rafts.
It is a useless thing, the doves
never leaving their cages. The clipped
ridges of their wings is an affront—the birds
pinwheel into the ocean, interfering
with a helicopter blade's hard whirl.

The birthmark on your wrist
reflects light from the cathode
as birds saw the air. Dawn
blurs the picture leaving ghosts.

The birds burn horribly, but even more,
the captain cries because the food in their cages
boils, smelling of sweet corn in a June from his childhood.

Our beautiful captain stands on the deck
and you're in love with him
because of his burnished medallions and his grief.
Despite the flaw in the television, the instinct to love
is the exact memory of flight for mourning doves.

Dearest,
we love similar failures: night's lost composition,
fire's leaf-like clamor, new light's stutter
as pigeons ascend to our rooftop.

The Devil's Book

1.

The devil is awake with his velvet pen.
Fingernails filed to points, he plucks

a blank white sheet and inks his name.
It bleeds through the paper. His apartment

is a miniature of mine, meticulously kept
and coldly academic. The books are filed

by century and there is no dust. I am keeping
up with him, my chair, the vertigo of a failed poem.

Bluing day. The frosted window is a lover,
a heart-shaped medallion in his throat.

The silver-throated man walks a cloven-
hoofed mile out of four in the morning

with a clickity-clack. Heels and cigarettes.
Zero moon. The devil makes me wait

but the night dials it in. Stolen
cars drive endlessly

fueled by uranium. Tires squeal
past my interior and the punks offer

names of all their childhoods. They are
little candles shifting in their wicks.

The devil presses his chin on my shoulder and tells me
to write this world, his voice raspy but soft.

2.

The devil shifts his weight from left
to right. His nimbus is a-kilter, darker

from the red robe he wears so early
in the morning. It is a difficult thing

to remake paradise. The ravens betray
this truth. They are shadowed seraphim

which hurts him like a tongue rent in two.
He dreamt my pen last night, and the moon

was a polished apple offered to the next
world. My note pad was laboratory white.

I was trying to remember a word
standing for light and rhyming

with innocent sex. Each time he spoke,
a candle flame flared, burning a crisped heart

into my poem. The devil wonders how long
he can endure in this dream of heaven.

The days drag and drag, murderous laces
against the pine floor. His paces

wear a cleft into the earth like a lie . . .
a lie, hungry and gaping.

3.

The devil rolls another cigarette. Thin papers
curl against his finger pressure.

He would rather the nighttime
and the illusion of godlessness

than a ravenous star. Easy
to see through the ink black

centuries after the fall. He is a grand piano
without white keys, all elegance

and bluster. He is no more the light
bringer or morning star, and his name,

a daily sermon. Dry lipstick.
Red filter. Smoke, a flavored silk.

Oh, to be rich with syllables, he puffs.
How they would cover the apartment

like the wingspan of a fat crow.
Heaven is his word. He knows he cannot say

"Let there be" and expect it to be . . .
his velvet pen cracked at the nib.

Aubade with a Book and the Rattle from a String of Pearls

The color of the trees is bleached at this hour
and you left a book on the table, face down
with its spine reaching for air. I thought

the book might hate you for that. With my pre-dawn coffee
and mouth full of sleep syllables I whistled the title,
held the book in my arms like something would reach for it
and carry it to another galaxy.

I would go on preaching to windows
about how the screens needed replacing, or
how the dust motes settle the shelves. You were in agony

yet you would not speak about things such as age
and the body gestures that come to claim your mornings.
Neck-sure, arm-sure, I think about you and your book
coming to some agreement . . . some place of rest.

Though the mica glittered like meteors . . . though you exhaled
circles in the dark of your skin, you entered
a slow recessional. It was a kind of starvation,
knowing the sun would come with its larks

and cars stuttering past your house. You in your bed
shut tight against the tide of sound refusing to believe
that the book held your world in such simple connotations.
A book is a book, you said.

I take that for granted sometimes. Perhaps
you were right to press its mouth to the table.
My imaginings sometimes take me
away from you. So morning paces

like an old man—mutterings of a book title
I've forgotten . . . tip of the tongue.

Each room carried us from clock to clock. Each tick
an earful about ourselves. God knows,
the way night moves its shoes from side to side
or how day wrestles syllables from us in our sleep.

What am I trying to say? Dawn on the spine of the book
simply stood for you many years ago. I thought of the denim dress
you had saved for gardening. You had asked if I could
remove your necklace. I fumbled at the clasp
and touched one of the ridges of your spine
as the necklace broke and the days fell around us.

God Essay

Torn asunder. We were torn
asunder. We were
torn asunder.

The Devil's Hour

The devil of my nights is a coyote,
fevered, starved for the scent
of rabbit and squirrel, his muzzle plush
with winter fur.

God, the moon, follows
over his shoulder. Snow,
luminous, turns jade green.

The devil's eyes are blue and I see
them glow from my window.

He's an unforgiving seducer,
toothy and lonesome.
Suburbia could care less

as he crosses from his world
into mine. The streetlamps hum and click off.

Darkness, still lord,
pads past my house, its head hung low.

Towards east, the sky ribbons.
The devil slinks back to wilderness, fur matted
with the blood of house cats.

Back to the low-belly, full on meat,
only to be ravenous again in the evening.
He fears hunger, his now-god,
who makes him howl. But

gods are famous for their silences.
so he will dream of his teeth in a velvet pelt,
licking clean his flank of all wounds,
all predatory injustices.

Aubade with Constellations, Some Horses, and Snow

Before dawn the horse-air spools
in the cold. The constellations mimic breaths
fading in their zeroes. This year's worn out
with lusts and grievances passing
from muzzles, vaporizing with Orion.

The house lights in the hills look
to be God with its windows all golden and heroic.

The little mouths of foals at pasture
snuffle for short tufts of grasses splitting ice.
Under stars they snort their own arcs of smoke.

Their coats are gritty and mean. God, they think, is leaning
his shoulder against their flanks,
letting them dream of hay bales and stable doors
unhinged into the liquory dark of evening.

Their helices of in-breath tick,
whole owls of flame. The field turns
like naphthalene—skins and snow.

Light leaves only the glittery skirts of white banks
clouding fence posts. Not memory,
though horses live in both worlds and forgive us.

Sweetness. The mind comes again with its arcs of sight:
and the man comes down from the eye of heaven,
singing pasture, pasture, a handful of sugar cubes.

Then the sound of gravel kicked into a truck's stomach . . .
then the clop of hoof on grass as if to say here is heaven.
Thus the horses forgive, though they look above.

Whorls of stars like thumb prints on glass. Winter's hard
romances airing out in sleep names. Ear twitch.
They waltz in their sleep to these names. Clover and Hyssop.
Names like tracks of serious foals nudging the ground till dawn
or the breath behind their ear saying simmer, hush.

Hoofprints pour down like color in dream while the night jars sing
to all the young horses of oat seed, brushes, and troughs.
Cold is sweet on windows of the house, leaving crystal skins.
Dust in the eyes and half out of mind, the horses tremble.
Shapes bent low, re-tracing steps for food. It is their way of keeping time—
munching forth the dead into air. Soon the sun will snuff out
the field like dust of a hand. One clump of grass
flat like the shore of another world. One star left snapped
like a beautiful fever. One breath like desire
rocked into the ghost of apples.

Penitence Essay

A blue flame arrows
its way through the globe of my eye.

Perhaps I was "pain" or had a broken knuckle,
a bloodied nose on the playground.
I've begged for it, but
I'll beg longer. I've been there.

I've seen winter childhoods
on the merry-go-round.
The holy light from the school,
jagged as the steam from the heat exhaust
quivers like tacky sentences
slivered between teeth.

It's cold. I beg you. It's cold.

Aubade with Bread for the Sparrows

The snow voids the distance of the road
and the first breath comes from the early morning
ghosts. The sparrows with their hard eyes
glisten in the difficult light. They preen
their feathers and chirp. It's as though they were one
voice talking to God.
                                        Mornings are a sustained hymn
without the precision of faith. You've turned the bag
filled with molding bread inside out and watch
the old crusts fall to the ice. What's left
but to watch the daylight halved by the glistening ground?
What's left but an empty bag and the dust of bread
ravaged by songsters?
                                        There are ruins we witness
within the moment of the world's first awakening
and the birds love you within that moment. They want
to eat the air and the stars they've hungered for, little razors.

Little urgent bells, the birds steal from each other's mouths
which makes you hurt. Don't ask for more bread.
The world is in haste to waken. Don't ask for a name
you can surrender, for there are more ghosts to placate.
Don't hurt for the sparrows, for they love you like a road.

My Dearest Apostasy,

My raven-colored mistress.
My owl-flight and letter opener. How you've grown.
How more lovely and tender.
                                                            More flowered
are your embraces. So wild . . . wild and extravagant
like hawks from a wrong continent. You've knifed
into the evening . . . dark hunter, dark tip.

Hello again. I've listed things whispered
on the envelope you've torn through: Rosaries and pews—
the corner mirror that belonged to you, though it lacked
my face. North.
                                    North you've chewed
a hole in the partition dividing light from light.
My, oh my, little dark one. Little she who travels in straight lines,
little wary puzzle, I've missed you. Let me say
I'm doing fine. Write back.

Hush

I was in love with the idea of the body in repose.
From the throat, a thistled song grew. Then
warblers. Then a mountainous trill.

The yellow breasts in orbit were messengers from god.
They said hush, for the body was god and it was
sleeping. Do not wake it and do not fear.

At this point the sound hurt as though I had eaten
a stone which became mountainous. It left
no option but to sleep . . . to sleep and become

more tree-like. More safe.
At this point I had abandoned my tune
for shade. I had become fearful and still.

I huddled in my stillness, though I loved
the body. I tried to mimic god in sleep
but the air was alight with wings.

Two

My Dearest Conflict,

Urged, I chose to celebrate the body
with rocks and stilettos.
I've hollowed the tips of my bullets. I've poisoned
the mouthwash.

Look at these hands—at the heart,
they're contemplating God. God, they think, can drop
a branch without warning.

Spare me
your sympathy, dearest. Spare me
the discretion of an overdone murder
or the secret of the sinister man you've willed me.

What good is it to be overdone without the rest of the story?
What good will you be with your hands behind your back
and your legs
                bound as in predestination?

Think—rain. Think—a man in a black shirt at the back of the bus.
There are eyelids at work here.
                                        Dearest . . . Dearest.

Let drive the rock you've sharpened to fury. Let fly the blade
to my suspect body. I suspect everything will thank me for this.

So thanks. Again, thanks.

What the Devil Said

Give me clove and tenderloin.
Hammer a bottle into powder.
Smear crystals in mud and call it
tongue. Say my name
in gasoline. Stun a bird
with a stone and own it.

What the Eye Said

I will give you my invisible star
and the gradual transition of horizon:
cauliflower light and cotton swab.
I will give you my ether, my other night.
And lay the shade in gauze. Not to see
the hostile in gradations of jewels
and prism light. My jewel.
My night, I will give you maples against the dark
and the loves of closed rooms.
I will be your invisible stone.
I will give you this road.

What the Scapula Said

Would I be the heavy fan?
Perhaps be the wing
                                        or fly?
Shake me, maybe drive me into
the dirt. Make me hurt like a love
or a toothache. Fling me
out like an archipelago. Roll me broke
and argue about rotation . . . give me the latest
crack at it all. Would I be your arabesque,
sculptured as I am? Would I lie?
Would I? Would I?

On the Pores of the Flesh

A partition separates it
from other bodies . . .
separates, but somehow still
makes it whole like merciful rain
beading on glass. The car's speed
jettisons the drop measuring
time and distance with the wind.
I have loved you like this.

Not actual love, but somehow
we've made our skins merciful
to touch. Touch, forgive me.
It's merely smart capture . . .
merely sweat off a glass.

On the Pulse Residing Behind the Lobe of the Ear

Quickstep and breathe . . .
each time I hear you nearing
there is a kiss that resides
beside my ear. Hear it?
Run and gasp little wakener,
little scurry and hush—
lips that touch my lobe
but only for a trice.

On the Fenestra Ovalis

Who has not mistaken the pulse of blood
from behind the ears as footsteps? The trot

of a horse with a burr in its tail? And who has not heard
the hand saw, then seen the cloth to cover the face

of the dead, dragged on the ground for washing?
To hear the grate. To hear the dog's nails clicking

on the steps and the blossom in a sister's hand,
her sandals sliding into the room–the butcher paper

she removes from a velvet box.
To hear a pair of blue insects with diaphanous wings

emerge from the velour, rubbing their glass rattles,
against each other.

Always the variable key—

in the distance, the horse drawn cart comes to take
the dead, the weight of the hooves

shake windows of the houses lining the street.
Always the latch and the scratched code of stone tablets

and the sounds that come from those who survive, their lips
looking for an ear. The living, they are not my name
or named in the Latin tongue of the body. They cannot be found
in the voice of the buried who have no hoof,

no blossom, no chord for a dog.

Aporia

1.

It begins with a trill for the afterlife—

When the wind blows open your shirt
and you are naked among the cornstalks,
certain rites have no point
                    in happening:
my hand on your thigh, dawn turned
                    to sparrows with their reedy throats,
my shuffle at the desk,
                    all my strains, forgotten.

2.

The truth is the mahogany of church
pews fill with a blue glow from open doors at the back.

I sit distracted, expecting what evening brings.

My God now, our reckless embraces.

This is more difficult than sparrows—sitting when the sun throttles
the doors to the house of God.
                    Children in the park
across the street sing. I put my hands in my pockets and rise,
                              fumble for keys and whistle.

3.

The year breaks like birds in a new orbit.
They turn and veer, swerve
into and out of the cracks of houses, tree limbs.
                                                  They dapple everything,
buildings, faces.

The riffling of calendars astonishes me—
welling up of clouds at the crescent edge,
earth indelibly limned.

The element of design here breaks
the way cornstalks totter the horizon's balance.

What an accident.
                                                  Birdsong wrung from the air
by withering stalks that deaden edges,
absolutes, so that the year stuttering at the boundary
of my eye is a yellow fever.
                                                  Look, I mean to tell you
birds in flight are a mystery not unlike
rows of corn blurring frantic into doggerel.

4.

My melody for the afterlife takes shape
from images my eye borrows: the wooden beamed church rafters,
your palm grazing my face, rooftops of our sunny
neighborhood left for the winged.

The province of my heaven is the world
tricked into fitting just so.
                                                  And just so, I move.
There you are listening with your head cocked, as though
                              lifted into the air an airplane punctures with sound.

A purple hue hems the sky, and around
fields before the harvest, you are my memory of the moment.
Day closes. The sky darkens.

The year breaks that way. Like a riot, Love. Like a flock.

5.

The sparrows stammer in their mottled beauty.
They know no faith
uncaged. You move among them like a hand through water.

You walk the hardening tillage, delirious in a long afternoon.
Forget the night. Forget the day.

It is only a space we travel. I say:
pass through morning
and cast a shadow on the ground.

The sky is a white-mantled line wrapped in
its own plans for the sun
as the children teeter-totter
or swing, moving in their own ellipsis.

6.

I know of two entry points to heaven.
One begins with a phrase I repeat.
The other begins with your shoulder in repose.

The light and the mahogany are nothing
but color and wood.

So are the questions we have for each other,
moth slipping by the window like an indiscretion.

7.

Our breaths are wrung from the air.

I am stepping on the top shelf of the ladder,
without balance. My wind the whiff
a nurse squeezes from a blood-pressure cuff.

Your mouth on my ear. Your eye, the trapeze artist
falling out of the tent's red sky like a scarf.

We are hidden by tall, unharvested corn and the world forgets.

Though maybe you are the sparrow alight on a stock
with an ear cocked for a chorus,
                                        thus subtracting yourself?

8.

There were always sparrows. Sparrows
building nests scuttling among the trash heaps
chitting songs for helpless gods.
What mysteries are there more merciful than the wind
blowing up your shirt in a moment of distraction?
Just know that when the doors of the church close
the only brightness will be stained by saints,
                                                the only song,
the hymn of children on swings or a breeze
filtered by husks of dying maize.

9.

What we do in this world
is not always our business.

Once, in the sky
a razor gleam split through the field and we awakened,

shadow on the farmland and a small plane overhead
dragging its dark double on the ground—
                                        a word to the lacquer
and the gaze of those bewildered enough to wake,
the sparrows rising from the crops with their fat syllables.

10.

All my sins, all my songs, you
                                        with your sparrow heart
and your laugh as I point
                    at the sweet helices of sun
                                        unhinging our window.

I've taken inventory of our things, and if I could
I'd repeat their names into the air: mahogany, corn-silk, laughter,
sparrow, sparrow, sparrow.

What the Ear Said

Nothing to hear in that hollow. Not boats,
not the cadence of boats and their oars.
Not wood and water and the ferry
to island in a storm, not rain. Not
the repetition of rain and the often loved
sound of trees. Or the sea.
Or the open mouth receiving. Not the lean
of the grief-struck against an oxcart or the low
of the dog caught in that rain. Again
the sound of the heart in the throat, and the too soon
lapse of breath. Again the beat of the foot
against the floor—the speech of the bed-creak
or the priest. Not to hear a cloak or some ghost.
Not moon. Not door. Not the entered shoes of a beautiful
stranger and her door, her moon.

What the Dead Said

We want for our signatures
and for the longhand narration of ghosts.
For too much talk of little. For the eye,
the mouth, for the hair. For the hour
and for the brush of that hair.
The nails. For nails roused
in unending growth, ghost of a thumb.
And for lungs blown empty
of the you and the you again.

What the Devil Said

Lo! A jigger of wine
fills itself to the brim.
Heat I give you and a fifth rib
crack. Dirge or prayer. Knife
set into a heel of bread. Feast!
Hallelujah. I've heaped upon muscles
a knuckle deep spasm. Ravish
the abdomen with provender.

On the Epidermis

Regard,
                the skin taut across the body,
its simplicity—something assisted like a corset

or a finger wrapped in a stitch. Here on the table
the body draped in cloth looks ominous,

like a thumb bound in string,
limb gone numb. How light

catches the loss of color. Gray touch.

The corpse wants to rule the shade
with its bald musculature.

To move
some realm of inquiry

missing when day goes to thicket,
thicket to the quiet
                                        and uneven blanch.

A flash in the eye.

This then is the benefit of morbidity,
the loss of wince, gasp
or in-breath from a barb-prick. That something

like a lesser of twin lightning forks,
something like the hammer

and the pain of a horse's flat shoulder
baring the weight of it's rider, gone

to ferret out

the fox in the bush, gone
to the haystacks we confuse with the sea.

What then,
for the flesh and the needle? What then

for a current on the skin,
this last pure quilt of reason?

On the Motions of Death

Upon death, gravity begins
to work itself into the body
and the blood's current slows
then settles, gathering
in small colonies, pools.
The front of the body lying on its back
turns the color of stone while shoulders bruise.

A man, minutes from death, told me
he could hear his blood leaving his ears.
I could see the retreat from his eyes,
the cornea fading to smoke.

The body does not die all at once.
The hair and the nails, though always dead,
continue their growth.
Some tissues live for minutes, hours
on the cellular level. Even the skin
rises, pilo-erection. Other muscles contract,
and in a last animal act,
the fingers of the hand bend, claw-like,
resisting the body being dragged away.

Epitaph for the Musculature of the Neck

I can tell you they were strong,
that they bore the weight
of the head and of the eyes.

I can tell you force
and of the light hairs.
More fully, the cold

and the grip of scarves.
Can tell the paths
of the muscle

from the clavicle
to the skull-like rails,
rails and the sputtering wheel-track.

And I can speak of their age
and of their descent:
bearded palm trunk,

black snag, laurel bush.

My Dearest Transgression,

It's been so long since I've seen the hair on your head.
Tell me, are the autumns as vibrant as they were
when I was in your ardor? Have you visited
the sites where we partook of the various trees
peopling your neck-of-the-woods? I miss those things.

Dear, how I've missed you and that greyhound.
Did you know there are gray-dog hauntings
around my neighborhood? Did you know I've seen
the autumns here, though they are unlike

ours and I think of you
with your ghost, nosing about the trees.

Sometimes I wonder if I've made my own
brand of mistake, though I know

we loved each other then as no other forest
could love a dog . . . as no other vibrancy
urgent as an autumn clutched to the heart of something
mercurial like a dog lost among the turning trees . . .

Three

Fury

In the village, palm trees against a house
make a clicking sound. The thatched roof caves
to weight. The rest of its shell resists.

Men will bring it down in the morning.
Tonight, with torches, hundreds search tides for children.
Each flame outlined by a gloriole, turns the beach a titian.

I watch the scene on television for hours.
The devil tells me to write what I know. So child death
is a cousin's death. The house is mine. The lie,

a deal known as memory. In the television scene,
villagers look to the horizon, faces red,
chipped like old frescos. Drama is danger

plus desire, a teacher said. So the villagers,
aunts and uncles, tear their hair for corpses
half buried in sand. The ocean is a frothy bitch

come to carry bodies away. Upturned boats
splinter against ruins. Poetry makes us bastards.
My dead cousins . . . my wounded relations

sleep in phosphorescence. A canopy of stars
endless beyond the ginkgo, shine apocryphal
on language I dredge in safety, not fury.

Aubade with Starlings and Kerosene Muted by Glass

I come to you
with the arrowings of a name
and the touch of cold glass.

Listen, there are names in the air
we cannot refuse. The starlings
with their bursts of color break
the clarity of horizon.

You say you are the bird that fell,
exhausted. I say I will come to you
by evening and creek. Be the birds
railing in the mistake of trees.

Thus we go on, myself denuded
by your call. The windows are preened
by our breaths. We are delicate
ghosts when we speak of this. Look,

look, you say, and I look. There is much
praise for the voices hurtled from branches.
Thus I am anointed.
                                        Idle with hungers,
the downpour of sound mocks the dawn.

Thus berries slash the dark.

On each flimsy branch, a song
                                                    I wanted to fade
like you on a walk with a lamp. The dark shifts
until the kerosene is unforgivable. I am unhinged by this . . .
I am unhinged.

Messengers

At dawn, they're within earshot.

They furl and unfurl. They glisten and shimmer,
radiantly tethered to the air.

They are out of reach. They are measured bursts, feather and lurch.

Then it's to tree stem, to stump. Then it's leaf to leaf
and mouth to hum.

They flutter up and out to assemble and reassemble what the sky was.

They are ingenious and distant.
Vast—they are vast and lonely. Lovely but measured,

they hurt to watch. Curving and lifting . . .
they fail to say, to do otherwise.

Otherwise, will the leaf whistle? Will they hang and quiver?

Begin the million things left to do? Will they green and reel?
Are they part of the topspin? The angle and hour?

I thought the swell of music is sister to the wind's lisp.

I thought there was an answer in all this, a story
and the light modified the story. They never come this way

after all is said and done. They preen and feel. They have such feeling,

their world so small. Like sleep without a god. Like a blossom
or a hum. They are hungry and they flurry.

Mysteries Essay

Uncertain where the glare is from, I stare
and stare. So surgical, the brilliance.

Clipped sounds from rafters.
Snipped and shaped. Something small in my mouth;

a cornflower blue stained glass? Hymnal?

A snowball can fit into the pocket but melts.
Who are you that would go on hiding things?

Gems? Bones?

Were you in front of me I would finger you.
From whence is the light? Can I get there from here?

My Dearest Recklessness,

We'd be in danger of splitting our loves into tertiary sequences.
You'd get the bigger piece and I would go on,
housed in my difficult sack-of-a-commotion.

Much like beach houses into the sea,
                                                                      we'd go on
with our difficult loving. Precarious, this stuff.
Almost too perfect were we not? If you, by me
were loving, I'd be an incandescent starfish.
You would swim the sea by my appendage light.
Glisten and wave there like anemones.
Capture and mouth your secret leanings.
                                                                      Were we not?
Were we not difficult and shifting with our tidy tentacles?
Do you not? Not to despair, you were loving and capable
by our common silica. Shine on. Shine—
terrible. You three-headed bore, I can't choose
between the salt of your tongue, and the two of you
I see when both my eyes are opened.

Aubade with Memory Crystallized into a Figure of a Dancer

That night was spent searching for a form of fire . . . the street
lights spilled off your face—the corner of the room

fully flooded with sapphire, a sticky flame. Earlier,
we had found a picture book you kept when you were young

and you wondered aloud, "Who was that voice?"
She had wanted to be a dancer—she had wanted to be the moon.

Such an awkward grace, to be the moon. Sky-bald,
abandoned. Zero and sleepless it aches and is cold.

It is far from fire, yet you crave it as though the rage
of sizzling insects, if loud enough, could spur the sun.

How do you fathom it then? Childhood singled out. Ageless
in your pirouettes about the sky, gravity-less and wounded.

And who would she kiss, I ask, and who would she ache
or grieve? And are you still so small and flickering or is it the window

who makes this mistake? Is it the body's battement and ballon that
vaults you
into the past, beyond sleep? We could not find your toe-shoes

among the childhood things you hid, though we kept ourselves awake
until dawn, searching because you had wanted them

and they had possessed you. They were just shoes but to you
a snare in the moment is everything. Nothing would convince you

otherwise. Not the hour or the way the hour begged you to stop.
Though this moment makes you that celestial body,

you cannot be that dancer, crystallized into the azure body
of that sphere's deepest crevasse. Though there were rivers

on that satellite once, the arch of your foot buckles
under the weight of your memory. The angels of the past

cannot be awakened through the turnings of a simple picture book
or the physical gleanings of the body recalling a moment

when it was airborne. Despite every aperture of the evening
turned to morning, this figure of you that you've memorized—

grande battement—would it recognize itself, flying, perhaps, or
    earthbound?
Even in daylight would she laugh? Would she flare?

Widening Aubade

And now the filigree of your wrist as it catches the dawning
moves beyond the room into the alleyways.

The man pricing a quarter rind of a melon pauses, light
ricocheting from his eye into a ball court across the way.

And in the arc of the orb's flight
from a child's hand into the hoop, the leather rotates,

representing the ever and the now beyond all sunlit rooms,
beyond the fade and the double-clutch which we often do when waking

to a new century, asking what we once were called in childhoods,
ever and now, for the suddenly and always that we wait

whole lifetimes for. And we ask for this despite the way cities
tangled in light slowly groan into the morning the way we do.

Dare your wrist become vulnerable like the stems of snow peas
snapped in the wind and the mornings will have succeeded

but to what purpose? Live out your colors to what end?
The scent of a halved melon is as remarkable as this. So too,

the thud of a basketball on the sidewalk released and gathered
and released again. There are whole moments

riddling to things coming to irrelevance . . . the body
lighter in its repose, the hush of a ball through a basket.

Somewhere, the moon reflects off the horns of an ox.

The horns are two shells in conversation, listening yet never hearing
a word you've said. But why should we speculate about other worlds

having not outlasted this one? The ox pulls a trundle through the dim
town and the men smoke and gossip about their debts and their women.

There is nothing special about this, only it is the evening of a funeral
and the ox pulls the casket of a woman who once sang beautifully in
church.

The men watch the cart go by, accompanied by their wives brusquely
fanning themselves and the children at their sides, and in an instant,

the decrescendo of talk revises what I once told you was unremarkable.
Gold earrings reflect light from the vigil and the woman's body

becomes a tawny reed. It's as if she's captured the change in tone
or the ring of the bell for Sunday prayer.

The procession will go on until our evening here, a continent away.
Our bodies will be white things in the sun. We will say anything

to each other. Perhaps kiss and touch and kiss again.
And perhaps we will forget the felonies we charge one another

in our waking and our breathing.

Elsewhere, the ocean swells and men who had been fishing

descend off their wooden crosses where they had perched
like little gods. They are blessed men. Later today, the ocean

will destroy their homes but they do not know this, for love.
There is only the mercy of fat monkfish and the sleep of the villages.

Waste-deep, they wade back to shore carrying their food in the cloth
of their headdresses now soiled with scales. From there, they look back

at the ocean and thank it. It is a small thing, giving thanks at the end
of a long day. And here we are. It is September

and the slight change in leaf color gives me grief, which is also small.
The air is colder and I have no fish to bring to you. Praise does not come

easily from my lips, and worse, I see nothing as provocative as ocean swell
from here, fixed as I am on the horizon. I only mention this

because if it were to rain today you would choose to stay in bed.
You would listen to my chest rise and think of the migration of geese

or the ease of men wading in the ocean. You would lay on your side and watch
my smallness grow smaller as the hazy sunlight erased my shoulder lightly with a glance.

It is September and the crystals have begun to form on the windows.
Earlier, you brought the heavy blankets out from the closet

and packaged yourself into a crisp bundle between them, sealing off
all the cracks cold could reach. Wrapped as you are, you are prepared

to hatch if the sun crossed your face, the only part of you exposed.
Here and now, the last of the summer spiders have crossed into our realm

and I was about to kill them all last night with a shoe, but you stopped me.
If in your sleep, they were to fall out of their webs, widening in the
    corner of our room,

I would take them in my hands to the window because it is your urging.
    I would cradle them past
the ruins of this poem to face the morning. Or,

I would nudge you from your sleep and tell you of the far places light
    reaches
when we are not awake. Those sunlit mornings of simple gestures

are what keeps us sometimes. If I were to wake you, would you be readied
to live in a world where everything important is small?

Where the growing nest of the moment couldn't possibly save us?

Aubade with a Heel of Bread, a Heart, and the Devil

After rain sputters to an end and there is nothing
but pulse—

After venous smells fill the room

like a gun firing. After steam and lullaby
of early-morning cock a doodle doo, I think

my name twenty-five times, a dulcet song
in time to the tune of the dog brushing his side

against the fence, and know it's the hour of naming
my ghosts. In the time it takes for the curtain

edges to define, I will mistake a heel of bread for a lung
and the Devil will dance off the knife-edge

jabbed into the crust. I will be a phantom
tattoo and the bone-rattle of ice in the trees. I will darken

and harvest, and you will know me
by the starlings and the killdeer and the crow.

But for now what the hell do I know? For now
I farewell the evening. Farewell cigarette and bourbon.

Farewell my devil with your blue torch. Here I am,
the vena cava, the septum, the shunt.

Prayer Essay

I was unusually ahead of my time with my own
hummingbird and my own riddle, like foxes' red

backs posing questions to the grass. I was strange
and blighted.

How do I leer?
How do I thrill, clay-faced, loving the earth
the way that I do? Shall I spare your ear
the brief wind from my breath?

But shall I give you no answer? Query me
or my snowed-in shoulder and I'll have nothing to say

except lisp, lisp, lisp. I have no blue eggs
dappled in gray, no stern reply for the foxes,

no sorrow or gaze. Spare me, for I know not
what I mean, sleeper.

Guide my dazed and head-long flight.
Flicker and stray, for the foxes
have teeth and our chirps are nigh audible.

Aubade with the Moon, Some Bones, and a Word

Half asleep you said in your dream you were a tree
and I disbelieved. I cannot forgive myself for this.
Though I can forgive the moon and the fish
that tumble forth in their lunar dreams.

There were light blue eggs in your branches that glinted
with specks of glass and no robins inside, only bones.
You took string and tied knots around the bones
to make chimes that would clang out songs
as though they were rain itself.

You did not want to lose the bones, light and frail.
You could lose them to the heavenly body with its fishes. You said
the salmon were there for temperance, though they confuse me.
They are merely mouths. Perhaps they are my mouth
taking you away from the reverie as I hear your vowels
and think to wake you.

The moon was a silver button, you said, and that a thread
was hanging from it, long and severe, unraveling
into the Milky Way. You said "unravel" again and again
as though you were learning a new language. "Unravel."

Slowly the night unravels like a ribbon pulled
off a bed-sheet. Scars are made like this—scuff marks
across wood floors . . . the orb and its string
becomes a swirl in the sky, generous rivers
full of salmon unraveling into the ocean,
your wind chime made of bones spools into galaxies of sound . . .

Little sleeper, little sleeve, I've become cynical as many people
who've become too conscious of disgrace. If you insist
that you are wood then let trees become more holy than God.
If you insist the bones are musical, then let their songs trick
the morning with its slow waltzes.

Ignore the fishes, for they have no real love of the moon.
Ignore my disbelief, for it insists too much on keeping time
and time wraps itself in your mouth like a lazy new word.

Gingerly, gingerly, there are cracks in our windows
and it's torture to end your dream as the sun dresses
you in vermillion. Stay asleep. You are a tree
filled with gems in the moonlight. Stay asleep
my lovely auburn sleeper . . . my beautiful burgundy wood.

My Dearest Regret,

You've found me and lost me again. How come
there are interruptions in your day?
How come the sweet grass and the hayseed? Pardon?
Pardon my leanings, I've wished you gone. Wished
you'd depart into woods, though you are the woods.
I've called you "thicket" sometimes. I've called you
bramble and black lorry.
                                        You're my dearest one-ton truck.
Were you with me at the chimney or the season
which you listened with one ear? Sometimes
I think you don't hear me and yet you stand there
like a signpost, like a wrecked chute for grain. My dear bramble,
dear black lorry, drive on. Drive past the field where the ruined chimney
scratches the sky.
                              Dearest thicket, you've found me out
although I've been hiding in the silos
near the field. You dominate the field.

Aubade with a Thistle Bush Holding Six Songs

A man told me that he had wasted his life. I did not know him.
We were on a train moving from one trespass to the next,
the fields in the windows shifting utterly into daybreak.

He told me about the guitar he bought with a little cash
saved at odd jobs, how he could not play but kept the thing
as a symbol for failure.

All I know about this man was that his hat sloped over his eyes
and the way he kept his hands close,
as if holding a sparrow with few songs left in its throat.

The rails below us were making comparisons
as if they were saying look at the thorn tree gone wild,
look at the gravel kicked on the ties.

I wondered about the hollow of the guitar and of the voice of the man.
It's always like this on trains—the burn of your ear
when a stranger speaks over the sun cutting through windows.

I was like ashes without feeling. I was like the worse wrong of pity,
like rain on metal railings. I didn't listen to his story,
though that was his gift. He wanted something brave

and so passed a breath through my ear, too warm for the hour.
I looked past the man through the window and saw three birds
on a thistle bush blur by, then another three flying from somewhere

and thought of the six strings on this man's guitar. Each note
the name of a stranger who's asked me for an ear. Each note like dawn
pouring through the windows. Some names rise.

Some names are left at the station. They can wear cheap suits
or drink sweet wine, but it's the story of the name—those sparrows
stuck to a thistle. And how they sang, how they sang.

Lullaby

Spill again, into knifing sleep
among dark curtains, long and rosehip-

scented. The easy slope of your chin
dips down into your chest. A vine

twists around the shutters. Blue glow:
a once-horizon spins its lyric

about you—dizzy breather.
Dim, your bough broken, you are never

afraid of my terrible orbits,
never scared of my hither and alight,

and the dread things of my worship.
Hosannahs sway nonstop

in the afterglow of dawn, too soon
coming, too early for sweets. Crows

gather quickly, arguing my faults.
My mind is awful and slant.

Murderers in the wings of the theater
and eyebrows, sinister

sister to my heartbeat
shake you awake. Retrieve

nothing of yourself in this pause.
Sleep. My lips graze your ear

and these terrors will drift,
swifts to lose in a sun shaft.

Other Books in the Crab Orchard Series in Poetry

Muse
Susan Aizenberg

Lizzie Borden in Love: Poems in Women's Voices
Julianna Baggott

This Country of Mothers
Julianna Baggott

White Summer
Joelle Biele

In Search of the Great Dead
Richard Cecil

Twenty First Century Blues
Richard Cecil

Circle
Victoria Chang

Consolation Miracle
Chad Davidson

Names above Houses
Oliver de la Paz

The Star-Spangled Banner
Denise Duhamel

Beautiful Trouble
Amy Fleury

Soluble Fish
Mary Jo Firth Gillett

Pelican Tracks
Elton Glaser

Winter Amnesties
Elton Glaser

Always Danger
David Hernandez

Red Clay Suite
Honorée Fanonne Jeffers

Fabulae
Joy Katz

Train to Agra
Vandana Khanna

If No Moon
Moira Linehan

For Dust Thou Art
Timothy Liu

Strange Valentine
A. Loudermilk

Dark Alphabet
Jennifer Maier

American Flamingo
Greg Pape

Crossroads and Unholy Water
Marilene Phipps

Birthmark
Jon Pineda

Year of the Snake
Lee Ann Roripaugh

Misery Prefigured
J. Allyn Rosser

Roam
Susan B. A. Somers-Willett

Becoming Ebony
Patricia Jabbeh Wesley